99 1/2
Food Jokes, Riddles, & Nonsense

Written and illustrated
by Holly Kowitt

SCHOLASTIC INC.
New York   Toronto   London   Auckland   Sidney

ISBN 0-590-93992-0

12 11 10 9 8 7 6 5 4   8 9/9 0 1 2/0

Printed in the U.S.A.   40
First Scholastic printing, February 1997

For Gwen Macsai

GOOD MORNING!

Why can't you depend on a bowl of cereal?

It has too many flakes.

Why do pancakes make bad politicians?

They waffle.

What do you call a bread slice that's been struck by lightning?

The toast of the town.

WHEN DONUTS GIVE THE WEATHER REPORT

LOSING YOUR LUNCH

What happens when you give tuna salad everything it wants?

It gets spoiled.

What kind of cheese do you use to build a house?

Cottage cheese.

What's chunky, white, and cowardly?

Chicken salad.

What's a good place to meet bacon, lettuce, and tomato?

A turkey club.

When do you pin a medal on a sandwich?

When it's a hero.

WHAT DO YOU LIKE TO EAT?

Plumber: Leeks

Garbageman: Junk food

Stonecutter: Marble cake

Tailor: Cotton candy

Acrobat: Upside-down cake

Musician: Beets

NICE GNAWING YOU!

What did the frog have for lunch?

A hamburger and a croak.

Where do turtles eat?

In slow food restaurants.

What do you have when you invite a shark over for dinner?

No leftovers.

Why did the rabbit go on strike?

He wanted a better celery.

JUST DESSERTS

Why did the burglar rob a dessert tray?

He heard the brownies were rich.

What's sweet, gooey, and fixes shoes?

A peach cobbler.

What happens to ice cream cones who fight?

They get licked.

Where does a criminal with a sweet tooth belong?

Behind chocolate bars.

What do good bakers earn?

Brownie points.

How do you take attendance in a bakery?

Roll call.

Why did the ice cream cone become a reporter?

To get the latest scoop.

How is a cake like a baseball team?

They both need a good batter.

Why did the donut go to the dentist?

To get a chocolate filling.

BOOKS FOR A HUNGRY MIND

Vegetables I Can't Stand by Artie Choke

Halloween Treats by Ken D. Corn

Really Hot Peppers by Hal A. Peño

Bad Pizza Toppings by Ann Chovy

Things to Roast by Marsha Mallow

Famous Foods

Attila the Bun

Elvis Parsley

John Lemon

Casper the Friendly Toast

DON'T KNOCK IT

Knock-knock.
Who's there?
Avocado.
Avocado who?
Avocado pretty bad knock-knock joke if you
want to hear it!

Knock-knock.
Who's there?
Beanstalk.
Beanstalk who?
Beanstalk, so don't tell them any secrets!

Knock-knock.
Who's there?
Olive.
Olive who?
Olive my jokes are as bad as this one!

Knock-knock.
Who's there?
Omelette.
Omelette who?
Omelette smarter than I look!

Knock-knock.
Who's there?
Orange.
Orange who?
Orange you glad I'm all out of knock-knock jokes?

DISGUSTING FOODS

What's made with ice cream, yellow fruit, chocolate sauce, and drool?

A banana spit.

What did the old cheese say to the stale bread?

"Baby, it's mold outside!"

What do you call it when a cockroach finds an old baloney sandwich?

Breakfast in bread!

IT MUST HAVE BEEN SOMEONE I ATE

Why did the monster put the cook in a bowl?

He wanted a chef salad.

On Halloween, when do monsters trick or treat?

When everyone's done bobbing for eyeballs!

What does the Blob take after a meal?

Bad breath mints.

Why did the monster buy Cockroach Crunch ice cream?

They were all out of Slug Ripple!

SMASHED POTATOES

Why did the farmer plant bolts of fabric?

He wanted to grow couch potatoes.

What do you call a sweet potato lineup on the highway?

A traffic yam.

When do you throw potatoes off tall buildings?

When you're in the mood for smashed potatoes.

What's the kindest vegetable?

A sweet potato.

BERRY FUNNY!

Why did the banana go to the doctor?
  It didn't peel well.

Why did the fig take a prune to the movies?
  Because it couldn't find a date.

What did the grass say to the fruit tree?

"Drop me a lime sometime."

Did you hear about the guy who runs a fruit store?

He's berried in work!

Pineapple: Honeydew you want to marry me?

Watermelon: Yes, but I cantaloupe!

Where do strawberries play music?

At a jam session.

What's purple and spoils a raisin?

His grape grandmother.

HAVE YOU EVER SEEN...?

...a banana split?

...a salad dressing?

...a lemon drop?

...a dinner dance?

...a fruit punch?

...a taco stand?

...a candy shop?

...a bacon strip?

...a baking soda?

...a hot dog roll?

FOOD IN THE ALPHABET

What kind of soup do you find in the alphabet?

Split "P."

What cool drink can you find in the alphabet?

Iced "T."

What sandwich can you find in the alphabet?

"BLT."

QUICHE AND TELL

What did the cheese slice do when it got a valentine?

It melted.

What did the Frisbee player bring to the picnic?

A tossed salad.

What do you call a stolen sausage?

The missing link.

Why did the ham go to the doctor?

To get cured.

Do you ever have food fights?

No, just table scraps.

Why did the police question the burrito?

So he would spill the beans.

Why didn't the burrito cross the road?

It was too chicken.

What do policemen do after work?

They raid the refrigerator.

SLICE TO MEET YOU

Did you hear about the pizza that made a movie?

It was panned.

How do you fix a broken pizza?

With tomato paste.

Can you drive a pizza?

Sure, if you change the olive oil.

What do you call the boss at a pizza parlor?

The big cheese.

COLD CUTS

How does Frosty the Snowman like his coffee?
Freeze-dried.

What part of a cake does he like best?
The icing.

What does he order at a fast food stand?

Chiliburgers.

What's his favorite salad?

Iceberg lettuce.

What does he think of frozen yogurt?

It leaves him cold.

DID YOU HEAR THE ON ABOUT...?

Did you hear the one about the jam?

It's berry funny.

Did you hear the one about the butter?

Don't spread it around.

Did you hear the one about the sandwich?
  It's baloney.

Did you hear the one about the egg?
  It's not all it's cracked up to be.

Did you hear the one about the cherry?
  It's the pits.

Did you hear the one about the hot dog?
  It's something you'll relish.

UNTIL WE MEAT AGAIN

Where do burgers get to dance?

At a meatball.

What do you say to a hamburger that's done a good job?

"Well done!"

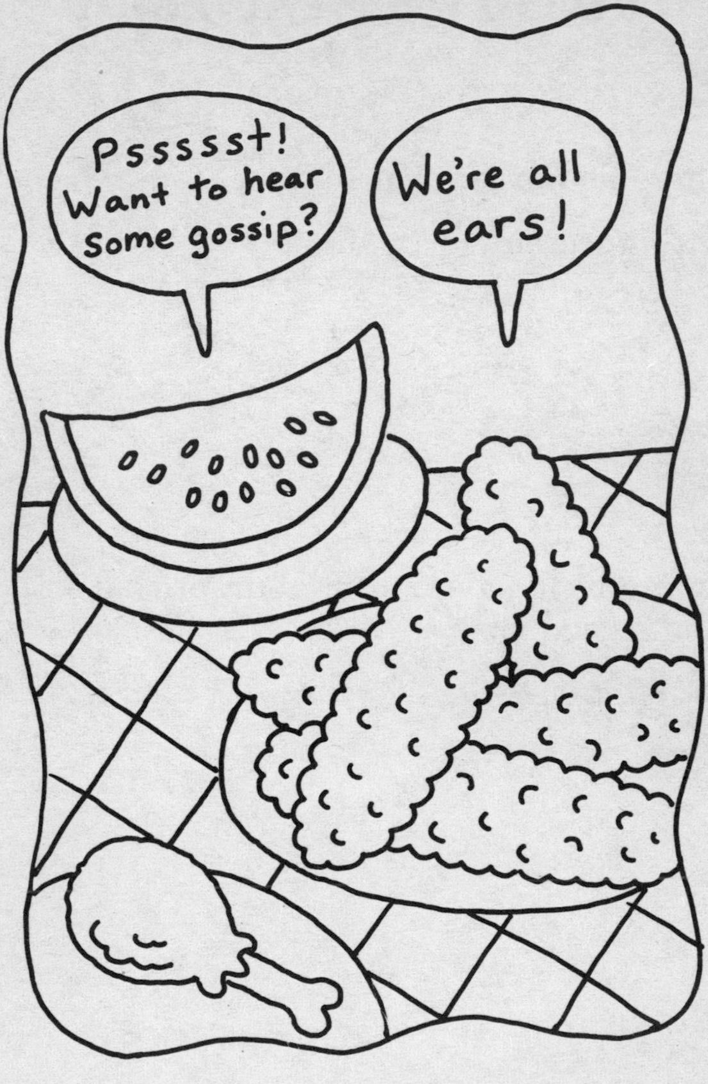
Psssssst! Want to hear some gossip?
We're all ears!

PRETTY CORNY

What do they serve for lunch in an office?

Corn on the job.

What does a slime monster bring to a barbecue?

Corn on the Blob.

BEAN THERE, DONE THAT

When do you give a vegetable cough medicine?

When it's a hoarse radish.

What do you call a cucumber that insults a carrot?

A fresh vegetable.

What does a carrot do when he needs a ride?

He calls a cabbage.

What do vegetarians need when they do homework?

Some peas and quiet.

What happens when corn kernels pick a fight?

They get creamed.

What's green and belongs in jail?

America's Most Wanted Pickle.

WHAT'S COOKING?

When you invite a clock over for dinner, what will he ask for?

Seconds.

What does an astronaut serve food on?

A satellite dish.

TALKIN' MUNCHIES

What did one hamburger say to another?

"You go ahead and I'll ketchup!"

What did one grape say to another?

"How did we get into this jam?"

What did one ice cream cone say to another?
  "Chill!"

What did one cucumber say to another?
  "Now we're really in a pickle!"

What did one corn cob say to another?
  "Aw, shucks!"

What did the bagel say to the margarine?

"Stop trying to butter me up!"

What did one lettuce say to another?

"Leaf me alone!"

EGGS-CELLENT!

What do you call an egg that goes on safari?
  An eggs-plorer.

What do you call a town of 9 million eggs?
  New Yolk City.

Why can't you tease egg whites?
  They can't take a yolk!

HOW'S YOUR JOB?

Tuna: "I got canned."

Burger: "I got fired."

Pizza: "It didn't pan out."

Egg: "They told me to beat it."

SNACKS AND SNICKERS

What do you call a piece of popcorn that joins the army?

Kernel!

What's a computer's favorite snack?

Salsa and microchips.

HALF JOKE

Knock-knock.
Who's there?
Donut.
Donut who?
Donut tell me any more _____!